# SHA...
# A BEGINNERS' GUIDE
# TO MAKING MONEY

'When I was a big star making lots of money, I needed someone with experience to look after me. Now that person's got the money and all I've got is the experience.'
**Doris Day**

'I'd like to live like a poor man with lots of money.'
**Picasso**

'I finally know what distinguishes man from the other beasts: financial worries.'
**Jules Renard**

'Never invest your money in anything that eats or needs repairing.'
**Billy Rose**

# SHARES
# A BEGINNERS' GUIDE
# TO MAKING MONEY

# SHARES
# A BEGINNERS' GUIDE
# TO MAKING MONEY

Thousands of men and women are making money from shares. Many started with just a few hundred pounds. Few had any previous experience on the stockmarket.

What is their recipe for success? You will find the answer by reading Harold Baldwin's practical and interesting advice. Then you can start making money for yourself.

WISEBUY PUBLICATIONS

# SHARES
# A BEGINNERS'
# GUIDE
# TO MAKING
# MONEY

Harold Baldwin

WISEBUY PUBLICATIONS

*First published 1986*

*Copyright © 1986 Harold Baldwin*

ISBN 0-9509751-2-5

*Distributed by Seymour, 334 Brixton Road, London
SW9 7AG. Tel: 01-733 4444.*

*Typesetting by MC Typeset, Chatham, Kent.
Printed by Lingholt Colour Ltd, London SE15 1LE.*

# Contents

**1. How to get started**     **13**
How much money should you speculate? How many different shares? The stop-loss system. Checklist.

**2. Sorting out the bulls from the bears**     **18**
How long does a bull or bear market last? Changes of direction in the market. How the winners did it. Checklist.

**3. How to pick a winning share**     **23**
Read all about it. All is not what it seems. Consider these points before you buy. Buy a share in the strongest group.

**4. Take my tip**     **28**
Tip sheets. 'Inside' information.

**5. Getting in first**     **31**
Stags. Betting on a certainty. Tenders. Placings. Rights issues.

**6. How to check the score**     **37**
Price. Cover. Yield. Price earnings ratio.

**7. The company report**     **41**
Profits. Past performance.

**8. Formula for success**      **44**
Constant £. Constant ratio. Variable ratios. Charts.

**9. When to sell**      **48**
Round figure. Sell in May and go away. Check-list.

**10. How to get a good deal from your stockbroker**      **51**
Dealing service. Discretionary service. Portfoilo advisory service. Commission. Clinching the deal.

**11. A to Z of stockmarket words.**      **55**

**12. Stockbrokers interested in dealing with new private clients**      **70**
Listed by Town in the UK, Channel Islands, Isle of Man and a separate list for the Irish Republic.

**Index**      **83**

# Author's note

Many of the ideas in this book have been given to me by
people presently involved in making money on the stock
exchange. Yet more are well-known but anonymous
market maxims. To all these successful money makers
and everyone else who has assisted me in the production
of this book I offer my grateful thanks.

If while reading the Guide, you come across some words
you don't understand, turn to Chapter 11 for an
explanation.

# 1

# How To Get Started

You can make a lot of money on the stock market, but it means some work, a basic plan and above all gaining experience. And it can be fun too.

Most people have investments in the stock market through life policies, saving schemes, unit trusts, investment bonds and perhaps a few hundred TSB or British Telecom shares. Many such investors do not have the time or the inclination to actively participate in the stock market, but nevertheless wish to benefit from economic growth and protect themselves from the ravages of inflation. This Guide is not for them. *Unless, of course, they wish to make a lot of money as quickly as possible.*

This Guide is about speculating on the stock market. Does the word speculating frighten you? It should not, because there is an element of speculation in all investment. People talk about speculative shares, but there are times when it is hard to justify even buying Government stock or a *blue chip*, a share in a large established company, on any grounds except speculation.

The speculator aims to outperform the investor by studying the market, developing a skill and hopefully finding the occasional big winner. It is not that easy. If you think that it is, or simply a matter of luck, then you could lose a lot of money. However when the winning shares are listed in the newspapers it makes you feel how easy it might have been.

Some people are tempted by stories of shares bought for a few pence and sold for several pounds. They have little knowledge of how the market works, how to start trading in shares, or how to proceed once they hold them. When they get bitten and lose some of their hard-earned money they moan about bad luck and put their depleted capital back into the building society. Or, worse still, they become desperate and gamble wildly in an attempt to retrieve their losses.

Obviously, the speculator takes greater risks than the investor. You can be both an investor and a speculator. You would certainly be foolish to speculate all your money. But keep the two types of deals separate.

*Before you make a purchase decide whether you are making an investment or a speculation – and keep your objective firmly in mind*

## How much money should you speculate?

First put aside and keep sufficient for your basic needs and insurance. After that it is a personal decision. Never borrow to play the market.

Move slowly. In fact, it is a good idea to play the market for a while without using any money. Buy and sell some shares in an imaginary way while keeping your money in a high interest account.

Be serious about it. Keep records showing every purchase as though you had given the order to your stockbroker. Calculate the total cost of the purchase, including the broker's commission (around 2 per cent) and the stamp duty tax (one per cent). Record your sales in the same way. Do not fool yourself. Remember you must pay stockbrokers' commission on a sale too.

Play the game until you feel confident, then tot up how you have done. If you show a good profit then consider playing for real. Also compare how your money would have done in a bank or building society.

Dip one toe in the market. Use only one third of your speculation fund and be prepared to lose some. Regard it as part of your tuition fee. As with many other apsects of life there is no substitute for experience on the stock exchange. But naturally, you should aim to avoid paying too high a price for your experience.

Beware of beginner's luck. You may start in the middle of a raging *bull market*, a time when shares are generally rising in value (more about that later).

While there is no minimum amount needed to enter the stock market (fortunes have been made from an initial stake of £100) in practical terms these days £500 is probably the smallest sum required.

### How many different shares should you buy?
The long-term investor should certainly not put all his eggs in one basket, but the speculator, should play for meaningful stakes. After all, if you start with £500 and buy ten different holdings of £50 each spread evenly over the market you are unlikely to pick ten winners. The most likely result is that in a rising bull market you will make a small profit over, say, a three month period, and if a *bear market*, when shares generally fall in value, you will make a small loss. In other words, the winners and losers will cancel each other out. Even if you make a profit the chances of you becoming rich in time to enjoy it are exceedingly rare.

Also, the more shares you hold the more time you must spend monitoring their movements and worrying about them. You can become confused, panicky even, and that could be fatal. You are like a juggler trying to keep too many balls in the air.

### The stop-loss system
That is all very well, you may say, but if I buy only one or two different shares and they go down I stand to lose a lot

of my stake. The answer is the *stop-loss system*.

This is how it works. When you buy a share you set a price at which you will sell if the price begins to fall instead of rising. For the average share the stop-loss price should be set between 10 per cent and 20 per cent below the price you paid. With actively traded shares in large companies such as Shell and ICI the stop-loss level can be reduced to between 5 and 10 per cent. A share in a smaller company in which dealings are less frequent or a more speculative share in which the price movements are greater would warrant a higher margin, say up to 30 per cent.

As the share price rises so you increase your stop-loss figure. For example, you buy Shell at 800 and fix your stop-loss price at 720 (ie 10 per cent margin). Shell goes up to 900 so your stop-loss price becomes 810.

Sounds simple. If your stop-loss margin is 10 per cent then you cannot lose more than 10 per cent of your stake, plus your stockbroker's charges. But you have to maintain firm control. It is easy to be swayed by other opinions and considerations. *The idea of limiting your loss on a bad venture is the most difficult for some speculators to accept.*

It is not a perfect system either. No system is. Otherwise there would be many more rich people around. Not all shares which drop 10 or 20 per cent go on down. By using this system you may sometimes sell a good share too soon and frustratingly watch it go on up and up. That is the price you pay for operating a safety net.

Stockbrokers in this country do not normally operate automatic stop-loss systems on behalf of their clients. The ordinary speculator must keep an eye on his own shares. The stockbroker will always quote you a price on the telephone and as soon as he has got to know you he will accept an order to buy or sell over the telephone.

Fixing the stop-loss price is a test of your experience and skill.

One of the chief exponents of the stop-less system was Nicolas Darvas, a professional dancer, who made a fortune on *Wall Street*, where the New York Stock Exchange is based, without ever going there. He had his own personal technique – but then you will appreciate as you read on that speculating is a very personal business.

**Checklist**
1. Are you investing or speculating?
2. Set aside sufficient money for your needs before you decide how much to put in your speculation fund.
3. Never borrow to play the market.
4. First play the market without money.
5. Begin slowly and beware of beginner's luck.
6. Decide how many holdings to buy.
7. Practise the stop-loss system.

# 2

# Sorting Out The Bulls From The Bears

Like many other facets of life stock markets move in cycles. When prices are rising it is known as a *bull market* and when they are falling it is called a *bear market*. Similarly, a person who expects prices to rise is a *bull* and one who expects them to fall is a *bear*.

At the beginning of an upswing, share prices react to improving economic conditions. As the improvement gathers strength buyers become more confident and prices rise. Eventually, buyers become over-optimistic, they only see the good news, and many people who never bought shares before are tempted into the market as an easy way of making money.

Too high a price is put on the future and inevitably there is a reaction. Optimism gives way to pessimism and prices fall. After a while the pessimism is overdone and a new bull market begins. This is an over-simplified description of the cycle as you will discover later. *But the bull and bear cycle is the primary factor in making money in the stockmarket.*

Before you enter into any deal you should decide quite definitely whether the market is in a bull or a bear phase. Then go with the market. *Never buck the trend.*

If the market is in an upswing go ahead and buy the share or shares you fancy, but if it is in a downswing do nothing. Keep your money on deposit.

True, it is possible to make money in a falling bear market by various methods such as selling shares you do not have and buying them later when the price has dropped, known technically as *selling short*, but these kind of deals are best left to the professional operator. The small operator is wise to adopt an attitude of masterly inactivity during a bear period.

The trouble is, when you have been in the market for a little while and hopefully made a few pounds, it is not easy to sit on your hands. This is especially so when you see the prices of some of your favourite shares drop by thirty or forty per cent. But learn to be patient and you will reap your reward.

### How long does a bull or a bear market last?

Answer: history shows that it can be anything from one to fifteen years. Professor Jevons, who had a theory that sun-spots have some bearing on commerce and the state of minds, believed that the normal time for the full cycle was ten years. His theory seemed to be borne out by the facts for a long period in the last century, but more recent movements have been less regular. The stock market stubbornly refuses to conform to any pattern and just when some bright spark thinks he has found one it goes off in a different direction and makes a fool of him.

To what extent does the market rise or fall during these periods? Answer: it is limited only to the sentiment of the investors. You will have heard of the 1929 Wall Street crash and the panic that ensued. Fortunately, there has been nothing as bad as that since.

However, in January 1974 the Financial Times ordinary share index stood at 339. One year later, January 1975, it had fallen to 146. Yet ten months later, November 1975, it had risen again to 377. Here was a good opportunity to make a killing. All you needed was the courage of your conviction that despite the dark clouds overhead the sun would surely shine again.

The Financial Times Ordinary Share Index which is published every day the market opens, is produced by averaging out the prices of 30 active shares from companies whose share movements are thought to reflect the general movement in the market as a whole. The FT-SE 100 Share Index and the FT-Actuaries All Share Index, monitor a larger number of shares and tend therefore to reflect the mood of the market more accurately.

The $64,000 question is, how do you determine that elusive moment when the market is about to change direction? You can prepare complicated charts. Or you can follow the so-called experts in the newspapers and on the radio. The trouble is that *the main characteristic end of a rising bull market is when the opinions of financial journalists, stockbrokers, chartists and other investment advisers are rampantly bullish*. They believe share prices will continue to rise just that little bit longer.

So, the other alternative is to use your own judgement. Your feel for the market. You know what is going on in the world. Take note of the experts, but why should they be more right than you?

The end of a bull market represents a period when nothing can justify the prices at which shares are changing hands. People buy anything that is going up regardless of the share's earnings or its intrinsic worth. *It is a time of greed and excitement. It seems that everyone has a stock market tip*.

You might think that these conditions would be easy to recognise, but in practice it is harder to spot the end of a bull market than the end of a bear market. You are carried along with the euphoria.

The picture of the final throes of a bear market is in stark contrast: black despair. Company dividends are being reduced and there is talk about this company or that going broke. Shares are selling well below their true worth.

The average investor is tied up with shares he bought in happier times and at a much higher price. Even so the future looks so gloomy that some investors will sell and take big losses. The wise long swing speculator has sold out long ago. Now he has cash in the bank and is ready to step into the market and make a killing.

## Changes of direction in the market

You can be fooled by minor movements or corrections in the market. The market does not go straight up in a bull period and straight down in a bear period; there are swings within swings. Often a sudden upsurge in prices will be followed by a fall caused by speculators taking their profits.

As a general rule a bull period is in force if the market falls but then rises within a few days to reach a point higher than its previous high point.

For example, if the FT index drops from 1350 to 1330 but then recovers to 1360, its highest point ever, you can assume that the 'bull is still running', the market will continue to rise. Similarly, if after a rally the market drops to a point lower than its previous low then the bear is still hunting. These minor swings provide money making opportunities for the experienced speculator.

## How the winners did it

Gerald M Leob, who made a fortune on Wall Street some 40 years ago, wrote: 'There is no rule about anything in the stock exchange save perhaps the one that *the key to market tops and bottoms or the key to market advances or declines will never work more than once*. The lock, so to speak, is always changed. Therefore, a little horse sense is far more useful than a lot of theory.'

Do not try to be too clever or greedy. You can do very

well if you stay on the bull for a good part of his run and jump off when he gets too excited. Nathan Rothschild, when asked how he made his fortune, replied: 'By selling too soon.'

As for the bear, make sure he has gone before you venture out. In his case it is better to be late and sure than early and doubtful.

## Checklist

1.  The bull (prices rising) and the bear (prices falling) cycle is the primary factor in making money in the stock market. Never go against the trend.
2.  Watch out for minor movements or corrections.
3.  The main characteristic of the end of a bull market is when everyone is rampantly bullish, so be prepared to jump off.
4.  In a bear market it is better to be late and sure than early and doubtful.

# 3

# How To Pick A Winning Share

How do you choose a winning share? There are over 2,000 shares quoted in the Financial Times and nearly 7,000 listed on the Stock Exchange. It is rather like studying the runners in a horse race – but with a far larger field. First you must learn how to read the form.

This means knowing how to study a company's annual report and balance sheet and understanding the various indexes and ratios quoted in the newspapers and magazines. In other words you need to learn the fundamentals, just as you would any other trade. Skill and inspiration come later.

Many people find analysing a company's records a fascinating business. Computer enthusiasts can have great fun preparing pretty charts showing, for example, price movements and resistance levels, the levels at which prices are not expected to go above or below.

*But all these facts and figures will not guarantee you a winner. If* success on the stock exchange was simply a matter of research and analysis there would be a lot more rich investors around. Do not fall into the trap of putting all your faith in statistics. Statistics are dead. It is what is going on now and in the future that really matters. The price of a share is based on supply and demand, not on statistics.

**Read all about it**

Read the industrial as well as the financial news. But if you see that a company has gained an important contract do not rush in and buy its shares. Shares react to good or bad news before it appears in the newspapers. The initial reaction could be exaggerated, or even totally wrong.

Before you buy any share you should discover everything you can about the company – its management, competitors, profits and possibility for growth. A growth share is your main aim. But it is not only you who must think that the share is a winner – other investors must think so too, preferably after you have already bought it.

You may spot a promising growth situation as you go about your day-to-day affairs; a new drug, a fashion house, or a food chain. 'They must be making a bomb' you say to yourself. This may be true and there is no reason why you should not have your share of the profits (provided their shares are available in the market) but you must do your homework first.


**All is not what it seems**

Many years ago I bought some shares in a company producing pots and pans at very reasonable prices. I liked the product – in fact I bought some myself. The factory was on my way home from work and I noticed that they were working far into the night. I even talked to one of the employees who told me that their order book was full and they were taking on more staff.

I lost more money than I could afford at the time on those shares. The trouble was that they were selling their products too cheaply. A proper study of their annual figures could have given me due warning. I had not done my homework.

Your stockbroker should be able to supply you with

information on the company. He may also be willing to tell you whether he recommends a purchase at the current price, but remember again that no-one has an infallible crystal ball in this game. A stockbroker's opinion, however well informed and considered is no guarantee.

I have missed out on several good deals by listening to my stockbroker. I blame no-one but myself. Have the courage of your own convictions.

The service cards issued by Extel provide another source of information. A typical card gives a summary of the company's reports, profit figures, rights issues and other important events going back over a number of years. Some banks and public libraries subscribe to this service.

In addition to the study of a particular company's affairs you must also consider outside influences. To give a simple example, if car workers are threatening to strike do not buy a share in any company connected with that industry. On the other hand, if a tourist boom is forecast it might persuade you to hang on to your shares in a hotel chain.

Shares move in accordance with supply and demand, but *in the final analysis the value of a share is determined by its return to the investor*. This depends on its profitability and on the value of its assets. Therefore, if you look for undervalued assets you must be on the right track – provided the assets are what people want.

If general conditions are improving ask yourself whether that particular company is having a fair share of the general improvement. Is its value rising? If so, determine whether the price of its shares is low or high with reference to its value. If the price is low buy the shares. Keep it until the price appears to be up to the value and then take your profit.

Some investors study only one or two shares, usually

blue chips such as Shell or ICI. They get to know their intrinsic value and deal mainly in their stocks, buying when they are out of favour and selling when they are riding high. Admittedly, this can be a fairly long-term speculation, but it has proved a reliable one.

## Consider these points before you make a purchase

Do not buy an inactive share (i.e. a share in which there are few dealings.) As a speculator you must always be able to sell as soon as you think it is the right moment. Sleep with a lazy dog and you awake with fleas.

Do not buy more of the same shares at a lower price. Once a share starts to fall it often continues on the downward path. A dried up cow goes to the butcher. Average up, never down.

Do not let your political views cloud your judgement. Moral values are a different matter. The Ethical Investment Research and Information Service (EIRIS) set up by Quakers, Methodists, OXFAM and other church organisations provides an ethical analysis of the activities of many companies. Their address is 9, Poland Street, London W1V 3DG.

Do not buy because you are attracted by the name of the company. You may laugh, but many people allow a name to influence their decision.

Be wary of the sure winner. *When you think you have a dead cert, think again.* More people get stung by sure things than by bees.

If the market suddenly rises do not rush to buy. You could be buying at the top price. There is often a reaction to a big rise. Buy on reactions. Sell on sharp rises in price.

Never try to take revenge on the market. This is totally wrong and it could lead you into a reckless gamble. Buy only with a view to making money, not with the idea of making up your losses.

**Buy a share in the strongest group**

The market does not move as one body. For example, the FT index may rise 50 points in a month, but the shipping and transport group index may actually fall. On the other hand newspaper and publishing shares may rise far above the average. Follow the Leaders and Laggards table in the Financial Times.

If you are playing the business cycle and plan to buy when you think that the bull is just waking up, go for a market leader which responds to an upturn in personal spending (consumer goods) such as Marks and Spencer. Later when the boom gathers strength switch to companies supplying capital goods such as machinery or engineering shares.

Remember, *when* you buy is often more important than *what* you buy. The market is in its strongest position when prices are weak and the outlook gloomy; it is in a weak position when prices are high and business booming. The strong have potential weakness. The weak have potential strength.

Do not buy on the strength of a message from your God. To quote Maurice Baring: 'If you would know what the Lord God thinks of money you only have to look at those to whom he gives it.'

# 4

# Take My Tip

There are plenty of people eager to tell you how to make money out of the stock market; city editors, financial consultants, tip-sheets. They are all experts and they all purport to be in the know. Why not follow their advice and forget about studying company reports and the state of the market?

A few years ago the London Business School carried out a survey on New Year tips given in newspapers such as the Daily Telegraph, the Sunday Times, the Economist and in some well-established tip-sheets. Their verdict was that the tipsters, in general, did slightly better – but only slightly – than if they had used a pin to pick similar sized companies.

## Tip sheets
Tip-sheets have enjoyed great popularity for several years now. They contain about eight pages, rarely more, and are published weekly. An annual subscription costs from £40 to £150 although they often make introductory offers. The sheet is sent direct to you through the post.

Some of them have been going for many years. Others have sprung up as interest in the stock market has increased. A good percentage of them disappear after a while, depending on how well their tips work out. They are soon replaced by new stars offering even greater rewards.

Their advertising can be persuasive, showing examples of tips which have risen spectacularly. They do occasionally pick a big winner. The law of averages could have something to do with it. But their losers are forgotten – except, of course, by the poor people who bought them.

The big danger is that they tend to recommend small companies, which have relatively few shares on issue. Remember the advice previously quoted warning the speculator to *steer clear of small inactive shares.*

Tip-sheet editors like shares which have a *thin market* because a small increase in the demand can send the price soaring. They can then say how wonderful they are. Unfortunately, the process can work equally quickly in reverse.

If you do take the advice of a tip-sheet you must move very quickly. Even so, you are unlikely to be quick enough. You are competing with the real professionals. To quote one leading city expert: 'If a share is tipped people are on the telephone by 8.30 on the morning the tip-sheet appears. The share may rise rapidly in the first hour of dealing, but by ten o'clock the game is over.'

There is also the chance that someone involved in the production of the tip-sheet, a printer, distributor, or heaven forbid, a contributor, has already bought the shares and given the game away beforehand. You would then buy right at the top.

Not all tip-sheets are irresponsible. Their tips may well be based on sound arguments, but one must ask the obvious question: if a tip-sheet contributor has a sure thing why does he want to share it with others? Why does he not keep it to himself and make a killing? Such generosity runs against human nature.

### 'Inside' information

This question of reliability also applies to the chap on the nineteenth hole of the golf course or in the local pub who got a tip from a friend in the city who really is in the know. Such tips should be scrupulously considered. They could be dangerous. Even assuming there is any foundation in the story it is extremely unlikely that you will be within the first thousand people to hear about it. These stories go round the market like wildfire.

In my early days in the city I had an 'insider' tip. I heard that a certain company had made a greatly increased profit and was going to increase its dividend. The information came straight from the horse's mouth – from a man who had resigned a few days earlier from the financial division of the company.

I bought the shares and waited for the annual report to be announced. Everything I had been told was true. The profits rose and the dividend was increased. I rang my stockbroker anticipating selling at a nice profit. To my dismay the shares had fallen sixpence. The market had anticipated the news weeks before and the smart operators had already taken their profits.

*The nature of the market is to discount the future. When the news is out – and the future has become the present – the game is over.*

I should have bought those shares two months before the results were due and sold them just before the dividend announcement. I would then have made a profit of over 20 per cent.

After the dividend announcement has been made the question is not how much profits have increased in the past year, but how much more will they increase in the year ahead. This may give you another chance to make money. If the price falls after the dividend announcement so that the shares are standing below value, but in your opinion the future for the company is bright, then this may be the time to get in on the cheap.

An old market maxim runs: 'Where there's a tip

there's a tap.' This means that tips are sometimes started by someone who is anxious to unload a batch of shares in that particular company. Rumour that there is about to be a take-over bid for the company is a favourite ploy.

*Never follow a tip blindly.* Buy only when you consider the share meets all your criterion for a sensible purchase. Then, if the rumour turns out to be false you are not left holding a dud.

Judy Garland once said: 'I was advised those stocks and shares would make me a lot of money on the side. After ten years all I had on the side was appendicitis.'

# 5

# Getting In First

A lot of people have made money out of new share issues. TSB and British Telecom are the best known examples. The city institutions which offer these shares to the market are keen that the shares should get off to a good start. For this reason they tend to fix the offer price slightly below their estimate of the opening market price. It is a very difficult exercise and it is not surprising that some of these issues are excellent value and become heavily oversubscribed.

The number of new issues, due both to private companies and state owned corporations being sold to the public, has increased considerably over the past few years, and long queues of eager applicants outside the banks which handle the issue have become a common sight.

**Stags**
Obviously, not all these people are long term investors. Many of them are what the market call *stags*. This is the term for a person who has no intention of holding the shares obtained in a new issue, but to sell them at a premium (an immediate profit) as soon as dealings begin. Stags have become so numerous of late and in some cases their charges so ferocious that the police have been called to keep order. Many speculators have come to regard the game as not worthwhile.

However, you only have to complete the application form and post it off to stand the same chance as anyone else of getting some shares, even though it may be only a small number. The people who form the queues at the last moment are mostly representatives of stockbrokers and other financial institutions depositing applications on behalf of their clients or speculators who have waited to see how the market is behaving and having judged that the issue will go well are prepared to hit it with a large sum.

The market is full of surprises and there is always the danger that sentiment over an issue will change suddenly, possibly at the very last moment. By applying for more shares than you really want, or can afford, you risk getting landed with them and incurring a fearful loss.

The shares are usually advertised for sale in the Financial Times and other newspapers about five days before the closing date. The prospectus for the issue is published together with an application form. Copies of the form can also be obtained from the banks handling the issue.

All applications received by 10am on the closing date are handled, but if the offer is oversubscribed at that time the list is officially closed at one minute past ten.

When an offer is hugely oversubscribed the smaller applications are often subjected to a ballot so that the unlucky investor will not receive any shares. Applicants for a larger number of shares receive a proportion (sometimes a very small one, maybe less than 2 per cent) of the shares they applied for.

In order to curb abuses of the system the issuing house usually warns that multiple applications from the same person will be weeded out and rejected and that all cheques sent with applications will be cleared before any allotment is made. The aim of clearing the cheques is to discourage applicants from writing cheques for a larger amount than their bank account will stand on the presumption that the allotments will be scaled down.

If your application is scaled down to say 200 shares and the shares go up only a modest amount a large percentage of your profit will be taken by stockbrokers' charges when you sell and loss of interest on your stake money (which is normally much more than the shares allocated).

**Betting on a certainty**
Some issues such as British Telecom, British Gas and the TSB receive wide pre-launch publicity. You can get a fair idea of how these kind of issues will go from reading the newspapers. It would have been a great shock if British Telecom had not been a success and small applicants had not been treated well in support of the concept of wider share ownership. However, these near certainties are comparatively rare.

There are new issues almost every week of the year, but not all of them attract a premium and only a few are worth *stagging* (buying for a quick return). See the recent issues column in the Financial Times.

Nevertheless, if you have confidence in a share you might consider buying some or adding to your allotment after dealings begin. Good shares often rise substantially after they come on the market. British Telecom was a good buy at around 50p premium during the first days of dealings.

**Tenders**
Another way of putting shares on the market is to issue them for *tender*. This is the same as an issue for sale except that the price of the share is not fixed in advance, although a minimum price is usually stated. You have to give the price at which you are prepared to purchase the number of shares you apply for. Applications are then accepted starting from the highest price offered until the

entire issue is taken up.

For example, supposing 500,000 shares are offered at the minimum price of £2 and applications are received as follows:

100,000 shares tendered for at £2.40
100,000 shares tendered for at £2.30
300,000 shares tendered for at £2.20
200,000 shares tendered for at £2.10
200,000 shares tendered for at £2.00

In this case the issue is oversubscribed and the 500,000 shares offered would be allotted at £2.20 per share.

Obviously, *tender* issues offer less scope for the *stags*, but this does not mean that they should be ignored. Most tender issues open slightly above the minimum price. Your best plan is to bid the price you think the shares are worth as a good short-term buy. You will not have to pay more and you may pick up a bargain.

## Placing

Small issues of shares which are unlikely to raise much public interest are sometimes *placed* with city institutions or through a stockbroker to his clients. Sometimes these shares reach a high premium and it is worthwhile keeping an eye open for these issues. If you see an issue which attracts you contact your stockbroker quickly.

In offers for sale successful applicants receive *letters of acceptance*. If the shares are not *fully paid*, that is you pay the cost by two or three instalments, the letter will contain a timetable showing the latest dates when further instalments known as *calls* have to be made. It is important to put these dates in your diary as failure to pay an instalment on time may mean that the earlier payments are fortified.

## Rights issues

Companies sometimes find it necessary to raise additional

funds for general expansion or special projects. One way of raising the money is to issue new shares to existing shareholders for cash. This is known as a *rights* issue.

Obviously, the shares must be issued at below the current market price or no-one will buy them. However, an issue to the general public on preferential terms would upset existing shareholders so the offer is made to existing holders in proportion to the number of shares they hold eg one for one or one for two.

Shareholders may then decide whether to take up their *rights* by paying for them or selling their *rights* on the market, assuming that there is sufficient demand for them at the time to attract a premium.

A *rights* issue generally depresses the market price of the existing shares, because some shareholders are bound to sell their *rights* either because they simply cannot afford to take them up, or because they do not wish to increase their holding in the company.

Apart from providing a good investment opportunity a *rights* issue can also offer a chance to make a quick profit. A comparatively small rise in the price of the existing shares can mean a big rise in the price of the *rights*. For example, if the existing ordinary shares stand at £3 and the *rights* are issued at £2.80 then one would expect the market price of the *rights nil paid* to be about 20p. Assuming that the ordinary shares make a modest rise to £3.20 it follows that the *rights* would then stand at around 40p. So, a rise of seven per cent in the existing ordinary shares is reflected in a hundred percent rise in the *rights*. Warning: the process works as well in reverse.

# 6

# How To Check The Score

As mentioned in Chapter 3 you need to study the form before you plunge into the market. This means reading the financial section of your newspaper regularly. If you do not buy or have access to the *Financial Times* every day (your local library will keep copies) then you should get a copy at least once a week. I find the Saturday edition the most interesting because it is slanted more towards the personal investor. As for financial magazines there is the weekly *Investor's Chronicle* and several others to choose from.

Before you turn to the news items, the reports of company meetings and the feature articles you need to know how to read the current prices. Here is an example of a share list.

| High | Low | Company | Price | +or− | Div | Cover | Yield | P/E |
|------|-----|---------|-------|------|-----|-------|-------|-----|
| p | p | | p | p | p | | % | |
| 204 | 180 | J. Sloucher | 200 | +2 | 20 | 2 | 10 | 5 |

The first two columns show the highest and lowest prices the shares have been during the current year. Then comes the name of the company and the price based on the previous day's dealings. It may not be the closing price, because some newspapers set up their lists earlier in the afternoon.

## Price
The price quoted is the middle price. There are actually two prices in the market; the buying price and the selling price and the difference between the two represents the dealer's commission. This margin depends largely on the price of the share and how actively it is traded.

For example, the margin on a popular share such as British Telecom standing around 200p would be about 2p, so the broker might quote you 202p to 204p. In other words he can buy for you at 204p and sell at 202p. In this case the newspaper would quote the middle price of 203p.

The next column shows how much the shares went up or down compared with the price quoted on the previous day.

## Cover
Then comes the *cover* which shows the extent to which a company's dividend is exceeded by its *earnings* (profits). If a company pays a dividend of 20p a share, but had enough profits to pay 40p a share then the dividend would have been covered twice. The higher the cover the more scope there is for the company to pay out more dividend to its shareholders. Where cover is less than twice you may have reason to suspect that future dividends are in doubt.

## Yield
The *yield* is the percentage return a shareholder receives as a dividend on every £100 invested in the company. This is calculated by multiplying the gross dividend by 100 and dividing it by the current share price. For example, if the gross dividend was 20p per share and the

share price was 200p the yield would be 10% If the shares rocketed to 400p and the dividend was not increased the yield would fall to 5%. Of course, the lucky investor who was wise enough to buy the shares at 200p would still be getting a 10% yield on his money.

The dividend yield is heavily dependent on the company's pay out policy and is therefore not a very good measure of the company's ranking. Remember too, that as with all types of investment the general rule is the higher the yield the greater the risk.

## Price earnings ratio

The last column headed *P/E* refers to the price earnings ratio which is one of the most important yardsticks used to measure the merits of one share against another. It shows how the company is rated in relation to the profits it earns.

It is calculated by taking the current profits (often called earnings) of the company and dividing it by the number of shares issued. For this purpose earnings are defined as profits after tax, less interest payments and dividends to preference shares. This gives an earnings per share figure which is then divided into the current share price to give the P/E ratio. For example, a company with a quoted share price of 200p and earnings of 40p per share would have a P/E ratio of 5.

The figure shows the extent to which the share price is supported by the earnings. The higher the P/E ratio the greater the expectation the market has that profits will rise; buyers normally regard a company with a high P/E ratio as a high flyer and they are therefore willing to pay a comparatively high price for potential future profits. A low P/E ratio indicates that the market regards the company as dull and unlikely to improve its profit record.

The market could have got it wrong and a low P/E may

mean that the share is undervalued and represents a good buy. The skill is to judge whether a share's P/E is over or underrating its potential.

It follows that near the top of a bull market P/E ratios are generally high while at the bottom of a bear market they are low.

# 7

# The Company Report

Companies spend a great deal of money producing glossy annual reports, but few shareholders do more than glance at the pictures and skip through the Chairman's review. Admittedly, the columns of figures look bewildering and the serious investor will need to make a proper study of the subject, but you do not need to be a chartered accountant to gain some useful information from the report and accounts.

The report and accounts are supposed to give a true and fair view of the state of affairs of the company and should the auditors think that this condition has not been met they must say so. Read the auditors' report and if it contains any criticism consider ditching the shares.

### Profits

Turning to the accounts, a lot depends on how the net profit figure is calculated. How much has been deducted in the way of *depreciation*, an allowance for the cost of capital assets which will eventually need to be replaced, and other provisions? If this figure is insufficient it could mean that the company appears more profitable than it really is. An explanation can be found in the notes on the accounts which are generally more revealing than the accounts themselves because they give the story behind the bare figures.

Do the current assets, money the company has or is

owed, exceed the current liabilities, money it owes? If not, the company may have difficulty in meeting its immediate bills and that could mean that it has to sell a fixed asset such as a machine or a building in order to pay a current liability. This is not a good sign. Again the notes are important to see how the figures are made up.

If you exclude the stock (eg items which have been manufactured but not yet sold) from the current assets and divide these assets by the current liabilities you get the *quick assets ratio*. This is known as the *acid test* because it indicates how vulnerable the business is to the immediate presentation of all its bills. The traditionally minimum acceptable ratio is 1.1 but the higher the ratio the better. Any figure below 1.0 spells danger for a manufacturing company. Retailers may often fail this test but this is no cause for worry.

## Past performance
Whereas the balance sheet shows the financial state of the company on one particular day the statistical summary shows the financial record over the past five years or more. Is the profit growing or falling? A steady growth is best. Violent swings are dangerous.

Are the profits running in roughly the same proportion as the turnover, or better still, increasing? More business without higher profits spells trouble.

The *return on capital employed* shows how profitably the company is being run. If the figure is falling over a period of time and is lower than other companies of the same type, you need to watch out. The ratio is calculated by taking the profit before tax and dividing it by the total of shareholders' funds (share capital plus reserves) plus loans and less any goodwill. To save you the trouble of working this out yourself, many companies quote the ratio in their financial report.

The *net asset value* per share represents the underlying

value of the shares if the assets were sold and divided amongst the shareholders. It is the shareholders' funds less goodwill divided by the number of shares issued. If it is higher than the market value of the shares then the shares are selling at a discount. This does not necessarily mean that they are a bargain. You must consider all the other factors especially the company's prospects in the market place.

Many investors monitor these ratios over a period of time and compare them with other companies. But remember they are merely indicators and a proper assessment of a company is a much more complicated affair.

An item I find of special interest is the number of shares held by the directors. To put it crudely I am encouraged when I see that they are prepared to put their own money where their mouth is. Their holdings and recent changes in such holdings are clearly detailed in the annual report.

The Financial Times, other newspapers and the Investor's Chronicle closely analyse annual reports soon after they are published. A study of such analyses with the actual report alongside will soon put you in the position to understand them yourself. Start off with companies in the high street, that is those you can relate to, and you will be surprised at the amount of detail you can absorb.

# 8

# Formula For Success

Another way to plan your investments is to use a formula plan. Again it must be emphasised that no strategy yet devised is a panacea for all-out success, but formula plans have the virtue of being easy to manage and offer a good chance of above average profits.

The object of the exercise is to *buy cheap* and *sell dear*. Sounds good, doesn't it? But it is not a magic formula for selling at the top of the market and buying at the bottom. You are unlikely to achieve fantastic profits using a formula plan, but you should not suffer severe losses.

### Constant £
This is the simplest type of formula plan. You decide in advance how much money you wish to invest in shares, for example £5,000. Then, at regular intervals of, say three months, you calculate the market value of your shares. If the market has risen you sell sufficient shares to reduce your holdings back to your original stake of £5,000 and place the profit on deposit.

If the market has fallen you buy shares to raise the market value of your holdings up to the £5,000, using the money you have on deposit. Of course, if you start the plan at the wrong time and the market falls during the first three months you will need to top up your £5,000 stake.

It is an easy plan to work, but your gains are obviously limited.

## Constant ratio

Here you decide in advance what percentage of your investment funds should be in shares, the remainder to be kept on deposit or in fixed interest stock realisable on demand. At predetermined time intervals you then sell or buy shares, regardless of the level of prices, so that the percentage of your stake in equities remains constant.

Let us suppose that you start with an investment fund of £10,000. You decide that you should keep 60 per cent of it i.e. £6,000 in good quality ordinary shares and the remaining 40 per cent i.e. £4,000 in bank and building society accounts.

After six months the stock market has risen so that the total value of your fund is £2,000 more i.e. £12,000. Your shares are now worth £8,000 which is 67 per cent of £12,000. Therefore, you must sell £800 worth of shares to reduce your holdings to £7,200 i.e. 60 per cent of £12,000. You put the £800 (less stockbrokers' charges) into your bank or building society account.

In this way you have taken some of your profits, but kept the remainder in shares for possible further gain. Having increased your fixed income investments you are not so vulnerable to a decline in the market.

Suppose however, that your £10,000 investment fund was set up at just the wrong time and the stock market fell during the next six months. Instead of rising by £2,000 your shares fell by that amount. Your total fund is now worth only £8,000 and your shares £4,000, 50 per cent of £8,000.

Under the constant ratio formula you must now buy £800 more of shares to bring your holding up to £4,800 i.e. 60 per cent of £8,000. You get this money from your bank or building society account.

You must buy the shares no matter how frightened you are that prices will fall further. When you follow a formula plan falling prices provide a chance to buy more shares cheaply to help make up paper losses.

You do not want to change your portfolio, that is all your shares, to restore the predecided share ratio too often otherwise you will cut your profits and run up heavy stockbroker's charges. In practice, therefore some followers of this formula wait until the value of their total fund has increased or decreased by at least 10% before making any move.

**Variable ratios**
There are more sophisticated formula plans involving variable ratios. In these plans you increase the percentage of shares in your fund as market prices decline and reduce your share holdings as prices rise. For example, if you think the market is near the top of a bull phase you would only be about 10% in shares and 90% in fixed interest. At the bottom of a bear market you would be 90% in shares and 10% in fixed interest.

Of course, you can do better under a variable ratio plan than under a constant plan, but it requires experience and skill to operate successfully.

The more the market swings the better you should do under a formula plan. But it is a long-term plan so do not sink all your money into this kind of venture.

**Charts**
Stock market charts, whether drawn on paper or on a computer, provide a record of share movements in a convenient form, easier to read than a wealth of information in notebooks and tables.

Basically, the peaks and troughs on a chart represent resistance levels. The top point is where more sellers come in sending the price down and the bottom point is where more buyers are attracted bringing about an upward surge.

There are numerous chart theories and there is no reason why you should not invent some of your own. Can charts really predict the future? If they were always right there would be a lot more millionaires. Supply and demand alone determines how fast, how far and in which direction a share will move. When you consider the many elements, hopes, fears, mass moods, fashions, political chicaneries and world events which mixed together help to set up the supply and demand at any given time, you realise that there is no perfect method of calculating this factor. However, charts can help you to build up a body of experience and knowledge which can be consulted and analysed at any time. Use them as a visual aid to your thinking. But do not put all your faith in the pretty patterns.

Charts of share prices can be obtained from: Investment Research of Cambridge, 28 Panton Street, Cambridge CB2 1DH.

Microcompuer software can be obtained from: Brian Millard Investment Services, 121 High Street, Berkhampstead, Herts. HP4 2DJ.

A book *Bulls, Bears and Microcomputers* by G.T. Childs is available from the Public Affairs Department, The Stock Exchange, EC2N 1HP.

# 9

# When To Sell

When the system you are operating, whether it be formulas, stop-loss, charts, planetary influences or simply intuition convinces you that you should sell a share, then do so – immediately.

Selling is a much more difficult stock market activity than buying. You tend to suffer from hang-ups.

Selling at a loss, for example, is a bitter pill to swallow. Take comfort from the fact that the quick loss is usually the smallest. One of the worst mistakes you can make is to hold on blindly and refuse to admit that you have made a wrong judgment. *Cut your losses quickly.*

A typical beginner's error is to sell a share in which he has made a profit in order to protect a share in which he is making a loss. It is psychologically easier to dispose of a good stock and take a profit than a bad one and take a loss. In general, a share falls because the outlook for it is grim and a share rises because its future looks bright. *Sell a dud, keep a winner.*

## Round figure

Another beginner's mistake is to set a round figure as a selling price. Many people are inclined to do this causing a resistance point just below that figure. For example, if you decide to sell a share when it reaches 200p you will probably find that it will rise to around 197p and then fall again, which can be very frustrating. Eventually, it will fall way down and you will have missed your selling opportunity. *Avoid the round numbers syndrome.*

It can be fatal to form too deep an attachment to a share. You read the glossy company reports and get to know the names of the directors almost as well as the people living down your road.

You follow their efforts to make the company a big success. Maybe they are starting a project in a part of the world of special interest to you or in an activity you know something about. The more you become involved with the company, the more information you receive, the more you tend to ignore the market in general and believe that the share will beat the law of supply and demand. No way. *You do not marry a share when you buy it, nor do you pay alimony on parting.*

Every shopkeeper knows that it is sometimes necessary to hold a clearance sale to get rid of slow moving stock. Look through your portfolio and have a sale now and again.

If a share is slow moving in a rising bull market or has not come up to your expectations after a fair amount of time, sell out. After all, your profits depend to a certain extent on turnover. There may be more exciting opportunities elsewhere.

Some speculators set a time limit and sell if a share has not moved up sufficiently in that period. I prefer a more flexible approach, but you should not let a share idle for too long. *It does not pay to keep dull company.*

## Sell in May and go away

This is an old stock market maxim. The market often drops during the early summer and picks up again in the Autumn. Many fund managers and investors are on holiday during this period and as a result there is less activity in the market. People tend to lose interest in the market except for sellers who need the money. Consequently a small amount of selling pressure can send the market down.

Do not sell shares at the wrong time just because it will help reduce your tax bill. However, see A to Z of stock market terms for definition of a bed and breakfast deal.

Bear in mind the maxim *paper profits don't count.* You have not really made a profit until you have turned your shares back into ready cash.

It is better to sell too soon and the shares continue to rise than not sell and see the shares slide, eating away your capital. After all, you then have the money on deposit ready to step into the market again when you see a good opportunity.

One speculator I know regularly looks at each share in his portfolio and asks himself the question: would I buy that share at the current price? If the answer is no he sells it. He believes in always leaving a little profit for the next fellow.

Finally, do not suffer sleepless nights worrying about your shares. If this is happening to you it means that you are over-speculating. *Sell down to your sleeping factor.*

## Check List
1. Having made the decision to sell act immediately.
2. Sell a dud, keep a winner.
3. Avoid the round numbers syndrome.
4. Don't fall in love with a share.
5. Don't keep dull company.
6. Remember paper profits don't count.
7. Sell down to your sleeping factor.

# 10

# How To Get A Good Deal
# From Your Stockbroker

Before you can take any active part in the stock market
you will need the services of a -stockbroker. If you know
someone who is getting good service from his
stockbroker ask him to arrange an introduction for you.
Otherwise, choose one or two from the list at the back of
this book. Tell them your needs, roughly how frequently
you expect to deal and the amount of money likely to be
involved.

For convenience, stockbrokers' services are generally
split into three categories:

1. *Dealing only service*. This means that a stockbroker
will buy and sell securities for you on a commission basis,
but not offer you advice.

2. *Discretionary service*. In this he will consult you
about your objectives and tax position and then use his
discretion to buy and sell for you while keeping you
informed of his actions.

3. *Portfolio advisory service*. Again, after agreeing your
investment objectives, he will supply you with advice,
information and specific recommendations, but he will
only act upon your instructions.

Many brokers distribute a regular investment review
to all their clients. It is really a matter of getting to know
your stockbroker so that you are able to talk to him on a
friendly, but business-like basis. Stockbrokers are keen

to have satisfied customers and are generally honest and helpful.

If you live in the country try a stockbroker in your area. Do not be put off if it is only a small firm. Size alone is not a reliable guide. It is the commitment to the private investor which counts. In fact, you may well get a more personal and cheaper service from a local stockbroker than from one of the big city firms who may be more interested in clients with large sums of money to invest.

The small country broker may lack the research facilities of a big city firm, but that need not worry you if you simply want him to buy and sell shares for you at the best rates. In any case he is sure to have access to plenty of financial information. Communicating speedily with the trading floor should be no problem for him either. Try to arrange a meeting at his office, if you can, and have a chat.

## Commission

Fixed commission charges disappeared with the Big Bang (see next Chapter for explanation) and competition may drive down the commissions charged to private investors. Shop around for a good deal – you could save yourself a lot of money.

You can deal through your bank, but this is usually more expensive and it could mean a delay in getting your order to the market.

All stockbrokers require a banker's reference and some may ask for a minimum deposit.

*Deal only with a stockbroker who is a member of the Stock Exchange.* All listed members are strictly supervised and backed by a Compensation Fund in case of any loss to the public through fraud or failure of any member.

You sometimes see firms offering to sell your shares free of commission. These advertisements are usually the work of over-the-counter (OTC) dealers. Although the deals are done free of commission it may well cost you more to deal in this way than through a listed broker. This is because OTC dealers make their own market – they have no access to the trading floor – and their buying and selling prices are rarely as narrow as the prices obtainable in the stock market.

Their advertisements to buy popular new share issues and other such shares from you are usually the beginning of a hard sell to get you to deal in the kind of shares in which they normally trade. These are mostly small or newly formed companies. It is really a venture capital market outside the rules of the stock exchange where there are a few big winners, but many more losers.

You should be even more cautious about dealing with brokers operating from abroad. You sometimes see advertisements in British newspapers offering *free* newsletters. These are a way of discovering names, addresses and telephone numbers and many of these firms are little more than share pushers. Do not be tempted with stories of huge profits. You have no redress if your money disappears.

**Clinching the deal**
When you give an order to your broker you will have already looked in the morning paper or on a screen service (selected share prices are carried on Prestel, Oracle and Ceefax) and you will know the rough price of the share, though you can ask the broker if he has a more up-to-date price.

You can give your stockbroker an order to deal *at best*, which means he will get the best price he can for you, or preferably a *limit order* stating the maximum price you are prepared to pay or the minimum price at which you are prepared to sell. If you give an *at best* order and the price changes dramatically before the broker is able to clinch the deal he should ring you back and ask you whether you still wish to go ahead. He will also telephone you and report details of the deal or say why he has been unable to make it. Once the deal has been done you cannot go back on it. Your word is your bond.

A contract note confirming the deal should be with you within a few days. Check it and be sure that it is correct in every detail.

In the case of a purchase your name will be recorded in the company's register and a share certificate sent to you, though this may take several weeks. When you sell the shares you must sign a stock transfer form which your stockbroker will send you and pass it with the share certificate to your broker. Your name is then deleted from the register. Of course, there is nothing to stop you selling the shares as soon as you have bought them – you do not have to wait for the certificate.

Keep a record of all your deals and store your share certificates in a safe place.

# 11

# A to Z of Stock Market Words

**Account** The Stock Exchange calendar is divided into a series of accounts. Most of them are two weeks long from Monday to the Friday week. A few last three weeks, especially when a Bank Holiday falls within the period. All deals carried out within an account period have to be paid for ten days after the last day of the account. This day is known as settlement day.

**Account trading** If you buy and sell the same holding of shares during an account period you pay only the net loss or receive only the net profit on the deal. No stamp duty is payable on such deals. See Closing deal.

**After hours deal** The stock exchange closes at 3.30pm but deals are often done after this time and the transaction dated the following day.

**Allotment letter** A document showing that you have been allotted a certain number of newly issued shares.

**All share index** See FT-Actuaries All-Share Index.

**Annual general meeting (AGM)** Every company must have an AGM each year, to allow shareholders to vote on the accounts, directors and dividends and question the board on the company's affairs.

**Annual Report** The yearly independently audited report to shareholders which must be produced by all publicly quoted companies.

**Articles of Association** A document setting out the objects and administration of the company.

**At best** An order to a stockbroker to get the best possible price he can obtain for your benefit as opposed to limiting your order to a fixed price.

**Balance sheet** A statement of assets and liabilities that must form part of a company's accounts.

**Bargain** The term for any deal on the stock exchange, purchase or sale.

**Bear** Someone who thinks that the price of a share or stock market prices in general are about to fall.

**Bearer stocks** Stocks which are not registered in the name of the owner. They are therefore transferable by delivery like a currency note and should always be kept in a safe place, preferably in the bank.

**Bed and breakfast deal** Selling shares one day and buying them back the next in order to establish a profit or a loss for tax purposes.

**Bid price** The price you sell your stocks or shares.

**Big bang** New Stock Exchange regulations with effect from 27th October 1986. Briefly, it means the end of the closed shop whereby stockbrokers could only deal with jobbers (the market wholesalers of shares). Now all Stock Exchange firms can combine the job of stockbroker and jobber in which case they will be known as market-makers. Jobbers are finished. Also the minimum commission on share deals is abolished.

Information technology will expand. A market-maker will be able to display his current prices on terminals accessible anywhere in Britain – and indeed the world. Deals must be reported to a central computer within five minutes by the market-maker. You will not only be able to tell what the latest prices are, but also the volume of business being done.

**Blue button** A stockbroker's clerk who is allowed on the trading floor.

**Blue chip** The shares of large well established companies. The expression is thought to have been derived from blue chips, the highest denomination of chips used in casinos.

**Bonus issue** A free issue of shares to shareholders in proportion to their existing holdings. For example, if you hold 200 shares in Lucky Days PLC who give a bonus issue of one for one you will receive another 200 shares. You now hold 400 shares, but you may be no better off initially because the price of the shares in the market can halve. The object of the exercise is to divide the company's capital into more manageable units. Also known as scrip issue or capitalisation issue.

**Bull** Someone who thinks that the price of a share or the market in general is about to rise.

**Business expansion scheme** A scheme for allowing investors to put money into shares which are not quoted at the stock exchange or the Unlisted Securities Market. Buyers get tax relief if they hold the shares for at least five years. The aim is to help small companies obtain finance.

**Call** A further instalment due on shares which are only partly paid. For example, there were two calls on British Telecom shares of 40p each.

**Call option** See options.

**Capital** The money used to set up a business. **Share capital** is the money which is raised by selling ordinary and preference shares to shareholders. **Loan capital** is long-term borrowings. **Authorised capital** is the total amount in shares a company is empowered to issue. **Paid-up capital** is the amount of shares the company has sold to shareholders.

**Capitalisation issue** See Bonus issue. Also known as scrip issue.

**Cash settlement** Some deals such as gilts and traded options are done for cash rather than for account settlement. These deals have to be settled the day following the deal.

**Closing** A deal which reverses one done earlier in the same stock exchange account. No stamp duty is payable on such deals.

**Compensation fund** A fund maintained by the Stock Exchange to make good any losses to the public if a stockbroker should fail.

**Convertible stock** A form of loan stock convertible into ordinary shares usually on a specified date, or between specified dates. For example, a convertible loan stock 9%

1992 pays a regular 9% interest a year, but you have the choice to convert it into ordinary shares in the company at a specified rate of exchange (e.g. 2 ordinary shares for each £1 of loan stock) on say 1st June 1992. In some cases you are given a choice of dates and rates of exchange. For example, a convertible loan stock 1992/4 could offer you the choice of converting to ordinary shares on 1st June 1992 at 10 ordinary shares per £1 stock, or 1st June 1994 at 8 ordinary shares per £1 stock.

It can be said that convertible stock offers a two-way bet because you continue to receive regular interest, but if the ordinary shares go up so will the price of the stock in accordance with the underlying value of the terms of the conversion. On the other hand, if the ordinary shares fall you can keep the convertible stock until its redemption date and continue to receive the regular interest payments.

**Contract note** A written confirmation from the broker that a bargain (buying or selling) has been carried out.

**Coupon** is the amount of interest payable on a fixed interest stock.

**Cum dividend** Shares sold entitling the buyer to receive the next dividend.

**Cum rights** A share bought together with the rights issue attached to it.

**Cum scrip** A share bought together with the scrip issue attached to it.

**Dawn raid** The purchase of a large number of shares early in the morning at the opening of the market. Often the first step in a takeover bid.

**Dealing** Buying and selling shares.

**Dealing for new time** During the last two days of an account it is possible to deal for the following stock exchange account. Settlement date will then be the one applying to the next account.

**Debenture** Stock issued by a company and backed by its assets. It carries a fixed interest rate and is quoted like Government stock in terms of £100 nominal units. Its market value will move in sympathy with interest rates.

**Depreciation** Money set aside to pay for the replacement of assets.

**Dividend** The part of a company's profits distributed to shareholders, usually on a regular basis. An interim dividend is paid at the half-year stage and a final dividend at the end of the full year.

**Dividend cover** The number of times the gross dividend could have been paid from the company's profits (after tax and payment of interest and preference share dividends).

**Earnings per share** A company's profits (after payment of interest and preference share dividends) dividend by the number of shares issued.

**Equities** Ordinary shares as distinct from debenture and loan stock. If the company does badly the dividend to ordinary shareholders is the first to be cut, but if the company does well the ordinary shareholder can expect to receive an increased dividend. The ordinary shareholder takes the greater risk in the expectation of receiving the greater reward.

**Ex-dividend** A share bought without the right to receive the next dividend which is retained by the seller.

**Ex-rights** A share bought ex-rights is not entitled to receive the rights issue previously attached to it.

**Ex-scrip** A share bought ex-scrip excludes the rights to the scrip issue attached to it.

**Extraordinary general meeting** A special meeting called to provide shareholders with an opportunity to consider some special decision or happening concerning the company.

**Final** The dividend declared with a company's year-end results.

**Flotation** When a company's shares are offered on the market for the first time.

**FT-SE 100** The Financial Times Stock Exchange 100 Share Index (Footsie). The index is recalculated every minute and is considered by many to be the best barometer of the market.

**FT Ordinary Share Index** Probably the most quoted of the three FT indexes. Also known as the 30 Share Index.

**FT-Actuaries All-Share Index** Index covering 734 shares. A slightly misleading title.

**Futures** Contracts which give the holder the right to buy or sell the FT-SE 100 Share Index for an agreed price at a future date.

**Gilts** An abbreviation for gilt-edged. Stock issued

issued by the Government on which there is little risk of default and an annual fixed rate of return.

**Gross** Interest paid without deduction of tax.

**H**ammering The expulsion of a member of the stock exchange because he is unable to meet his commitments.

**Hedge** A means of insuring the risk.

**I**ndex **linked gilt** Government stock with interest and final redemption payment tied to the Retail Price Index.

**Institutions** A term used to cover all the insurance companies, banks, building societies, unit trusts, investment trusts, pension funds and similar large investment organisations. Institutional buying or support is sometimes given as a reason for a share's rise.

**Investment club** A club where people meet to talk about investments and to capitalise on the skills and knowledge of the members. If you are interested in joining one of these clubs contact the National Association of Investment Clubs, Halifax House, 5, Fenwick Street, Liverpool L12 0PR.

**Investment Trust** A company which invests in shares. It differs from a unit trust because its own shares are quoted on the stock exchange. To discover more about Investment Trusts contact the Association of Investment Trust Companies, Park House (6th Floor), 16 Finsbury Circus, London EC2M 7JJ.

**J**obber Someone who deals in shares for a broker, but his function ceased on 27th October 1986. See Big Bang.

**Limit order** An order to a stockbroker specifying a price limit so that the deal can only be done at that price or better.

**Liquidation** The conversion of assets into cash.

**Listed company** A company whose shares have been listed and are dealt on the Stock Exchange.

**Loan stock** Stock bearing a fixed rate of interest. Unlike debenture stock it need not be secured by assets.

**Long** Someone holding shares can be said to be long of them.

**Longs** When used in connection with stocks it refers to long-dated stocks with maturity dates of fifteen years and more.

**Market-maker** New name for a broker who fixes the price of stocks and shares.

**Medium term** Refers to stock with maturity dates of five to fifteen years.

**Middle price** Halfway between the bid and offer price.

**Net asset value** The value of a company after all debts have been paid expressed in pence per share.

**New issue** A company coming to the market for the first time.

**New time** See dealing for new time.

**Nominee** Someone acting on another's behalf. Shares

may be registered in the name of a nominee rather than in your own name to allow the nominee to manage them for you (i.e. deal with rights issues etc.). This service can be very useful if you live abroad or are often away from home. Banks sometimes insist that you transfer your shares into the name of their nominee company if you offer them as security for a loan. The bank is then able to sell the shares if you fail to repay the loan.

**Nominal value** The face value of a share or stock as opposed to its market value, also called par value.

**Offer price** The price at which you can buy stocks and shares.

**Options** The right to buy (**call option**) or sell (**put option**) a specified share at a specified price within a specified period. For this privilege you pay **option money**. There is no obligation for you to buy or sell the shares. You can let the option lapse if you wish. Example: You pay 20p per share for a three months' call option on Lucky Day shares at 265p, being the price at which they are standing in the market at present. During the next three months the shares rise to 305p so you take up your option to buy at 265p and make a net profit of around 20p a share. Alternatively, if the shares fall to 250p you do not take up your option, but lose 20p per share.

A *double option* gives the right to buy or sell a share. A *traded option* is an option which itself can be traded throughout the course of its life.

Traded option prices are quoted in the *Financial Times*. For further information and literature contact the Options Development Group, The Stock Exchange, London EC2N 1HP.

The main attraction of options is that you limit your

risks but not your rewards. The rule is if you see a good profit, take it quickly. Do not play with options unless you can lose your entire option premium and still afford a holiday on the French Riviera.

**Ordinary share** A share on which the dividends vary in amount depending on the decision of the directors and based on the profitability of the company.

**Over the counter market (OTC)** A market outside the stock exchange in which small companies are able to raise money by issuing shares to the public. Very risky.

**Par** The nominal value of a stock or share.

**Partly paid** Shares which have been only partly paid for and on which further payment or payments are due.

**Penny shares** Shares with a market value of less than 10p to 50p.

**Plc** Public Limited Company (previously Ltd). Private limited companies are still Ltd so you can now tell the difference. Some Plc companies are not quoted on the Stock Exchange.

**Placing** The sale of a large number of shares in one company by arrangement direct to institutions and others without going through the market.

**Portfolio** A selection of shares held by an individual or a fund.

**Preference share** A share giving a fixed rate of dividend. The dividend ranks ahead of ordinary shares, but below debentures and loan stock.

**Price-earnings ratio (P/E)** This is calculated by taking

the current earnings (profits after certain deductions) of the company and dividing them by the number of shares issued. This gives the earnings by share figure. It is then divided into the current share price which gives the P/E ratio. See also Earnings per share.

**Prospectus** An independently audited document detailing a company's financial history and current situation and published ahead of a new share issue.

**Proxy** Someone who votes on your behalf if you cannot attend a shareholders' meeting. You can tell your proxy how to vote or let him make up his own mind.

**Quoted** A share listed on the stock exchange.

**Redemption** The date when the nominal value of a stock will be repaid to the holder.

**Redemption yield** The yearly return you get from a fixed interest stock which you hold until it is redeemed. It consists of two parts: the interest, often after tax, and the averaged out difference between what you paid and the value at redemption.

**Registered stock** Stock in which the name of the holder is listed in the company's register and the stock is transferable only by his signature on a stock transfer form as opposed to bearer stock which is transferable by delivery.

**Renunciation** The giving up of the right to be registered as the holder of a new issue, enabling the issue to be transferred to another.

**Rights issue** The issue of extra shares to existing shareholders, usually at a preferential price.

**Scrip issue** Same as Bonus issue.

**Settlement day** The day on which all deals for a stock exchange account period must be settled.

**Securities** A general term for stocks and shares.

**Share certificate** An official document issued by the company stating the name of the shareholder and the number of shares owned.

**Share perks** A number of companies give benefits to their shareholders. These include discounts on wine, clothes, holidays, dry-cleaning and light fittings.

**Short** If you sell a stock which you do not own you are said to be selling short.

**Shorts** Government stock due for repayment within five years.

**Spread** The difference between the buying and the selling price. Or a variety of investments.

**Stag** Someone who applies for shares in a new issue with the intention of selling them immediately at a profit.

**Stale bull** Someone who has bought shares in anticipation of a quick rise which has not materialised.

**Stamp duty** A UK tax levied on the purchase of shares with the exception of Government stock and new issues.

**Stock** A security giving a fixed rate of interest for a fixed period.

**Striking price** The price at which an option is granted. See Options.

**Sweetener** A high-yielding stock or share included in a portfolio to raise the average yield overall.

**Switch** The purchase and sale of investments carried out at the same time to change the composition of the portfolio.

**Take-Over** One company obtaining control of another by obtaining a majority of the voting shares.

**Tap stock** Government stock offered for sale by the Government, sometimes to influence the price.

**Tender** An issue of stocks or shares where prospective buyers specify the price they are willing to pay. The shares are then offered to the highest bidders.

**Traded option** See Options.

**Underwriter** Someone, usually a city institution, who agrees to buy any shares in a new issue not purchased by the public.

**Unit trust** A portfolio of various investments divided into units and managed by professionals. The value of the units does not depend on supply and demand but on the underlying value of the portfolio. For more information contact the Unit Trust Association, Park House, 16 Finsbury Circus, London EC2M 7JP. Tel: 01-638 3071.

**Unlisted Securities Market (USM)** The stock exchange market for companies who do not qualify or do not wish a full listing. A sort of second-tier market consisting mainly of small companies or recently formed companies. If you pick a winner you could do very well, but it is a high risk investment.

**Unsecured loan stock** A fixed interest stock not secured by assets.

**W**arrant A negotiable right to subscribe for stocks or shares at some time in the future. Similar to an option but used by companies to raise money.

**Y**earlings Bonds issued for twelve months mostly by local authorities.

**Yield** The gross dividend expressed as a percentage of the share price.

# 12

# Stockbrokers

The following is a list by Town of stockbrokers in the UK and Ireland who are interested in new private clients. They may not all necessarily want to deal with investors who have only £500 or £1,000 to invest though many will – particularly those outside London.

**ABERDEEN**
**Horne & Mackinnon**
60 Union Street, Aberdeen AB9 1DH. Tel: 0224-640222.

**Parsons & Co**
25 Albyn Place, Aberdeen AB1 1YL. Tel: 0224-589345.

**William Murray**
1 Albyn Terrace, Aberdeen AB9 1RU. Tel: 0224-641307.

**ALTRINCHAM**
**Charterhouse Tilney Ltd**
Ashley House, Ashley Road, Altrincham WA14 2DW. Tel: 061-941 4772.

**BANGOR**
**R A Coleman & Co**
204 High Street, Bangor, Gwynedd LL57 1NY. Tel: 0248-353242.

**BATH**
**Godfray Derby & Co**
1 Northumberland Buildings, Queen Square, Bath, Avon BA1 2JB. Tel: 0225-337100.

**BARNSLEY**
**Stancliffe Ltd**
23 Regent Street, Barnsley, S Yorkshire S70 2HH. Tel: 0226-282277/282268.

**BARNSTABLE**
**Milton Mortimer & Co**
74 High Street, Barnstable, Devon EX31 1HP. Tel: 0271-71199.

**BEDFORD**
**R N McKean & Co**
11 Grove Place, Bedford MK40 3GG. Tel: 0234-51131.

**BELFAST**
**W M F Coates & Co**
Northern Bank House, 8/9 Donegall Square, N Belfast BT1 5LX. Tel: 0232-223456.

**Josias Cunningham & Co**
2 Bridge Street, Belfast BT1 1NX. Tel: 0232-246005.

**Laing & Cruickshank**
St George's House, 99/101 High Street, Belfast BT1 2AH. Tel: 0232-221002.

## BIRMINGHAM
### Chambers & Remington
Canterbury House, 85 Newhall Street, Birmingham B3 1LS. Tel: 021-236 2577.

### F H F Market Makers Ltd
Charles House, 148/149 Great Charles Street, Birmingham B3 3HT. Tel: 021-236 2211.

### Gilbert Jeffs & Co
14 Bennetts Hill, Birmingham B2 5SE. Tel: 021-643 7861/7507.

### Griffiths & Lamb
York House, 38 Great Charles Street, Queensway, Birmingham B3 3GY. Tel: 021-236 6641.

### Harris Allday Lea & Brooks
33 Great Charles Street, Birmingham B3 3JN. Tel: 021-233 1222.

### Murray & Co
Beaufort House, 94 Newhall Street, Birmingham B3 1PE. Tel: 021-236 0891.

### Roy Great James & Co
33 Charles Street, Queensway, Birmingham B3 3JS. Tel: 021-236 8131.

### Sabin Bacon White & Co
33 Great Charles Street, Queensway, Birmingham B3 3JW. Tel: 021-236 5591.

### Smith Keen Cutler
Exchange Buildings, Stephenson Place, Birmingham B2 4NN. Tel: 021-643 9977.

### Albert E Sharp & Co
Edmund House, 12 Newhall Street, Birmingham B3 3ER. Tel: 021-236 5801.

### Stock Beech & Co
Lloyds Bank Chambers, 75 Edmund Street, Birmingham B3 3HL. Tel: 021-233 3211.

## BLACKPOOL
### James Brearley & Sons
PO Box 34, 31 King Street, Blackpool FY1 3DQ. Tel: 0253-21474.

### Marsden W Hargreave, Hale & Co
PO Box 7, 8 Springfield Road, Blackpool FY1 1QN. Tel: 0253-21575.

## BOLTON
### Llewellyan, Greenhalgh & Co
20 Mawdsley Street, Bolton BL1 1LF. Tel: 0204-21697.

## BOURNEMOUTH
### Farley & Thompson
Pine Grange, Bath Road, Bournemouth BH1 2NU. Tel: 0202-26277.

### Godfray Derby & Co
Jacey House, The Lansdowne, Bournemouth BH1 2PP. Tel: 0202-25682.

### I A Pritchard Ltd
National Westminster Bank Building, 1 Richmond Hill, The Square, Bournemouth BH2 6HW. Tel: 0202-297035.

### Robson Cotterell Ltd
Bourne Chambers, St Peters Road, Bournemouth BH1 2JX. Tel: 0202-27581.

## BRADFORD
### Rensburg & Co
Broadway House, 9 Bank Street, Bradford BD1 1HU. Tel: 0274-729406.

**BRISTOL**
**Heseltine Moss & Co**
Stock Exchange Buildings, 34 St Nicholas Street, Bristol BS1 1TW. Tel: 0272-276521.

**Hillman Catford Board & Co**
45 St Nicholas Street, Bristol BS1 1TX. Tel: 0272-291352/24051.

**Laws Queen & Coo**
30 Charlotte Street, Bristol BS1 4DU. Tel: 0272-293901.

**Stock Beech & Co**
The Bristol & West Building, Broad Quay, Bristol BS1 4DD. Tel: 0272-20051.

**CAMBRIDGE**
**Charles Stanley & Co**
9 Pembroke Street, Cambridge CB2 3QY. Tel: 0223-316726.

**CARDIFF**
**Heseltine Moss & Co**
Pork House, Greyfriars Road, Cardiff CF1 3LB. Tel: 0222-377061.

**Lyddon & Co**
113 Bute Street, Cardiff CF1 1QS. Tel: 0222-48000.

**Murray & Co Stockbrokers Ltd**
Westgate House, Westgate Street, Cardiff CF1 1DD. Tel: 0222-397672.

**CARLISLE**
**Stancliffe Ltd**
1 Cecil Street, Carlisle CA1 1NL. Tel: 0228-21200.

**CHELTENHAM**
**Henderson Crosthwaite & Co**
25 Imperial Square, Cheltenham GL50 1QZ. Tel: 0242-514756.

**Heseltine Moss & Co**
2 Imperial Square, Cheltenham GL50 1QB. Tel: 0242-571571.

**Vivian Gray & Co**
Harley House, 29 Cambray Place, Cheltenham GL50 1JN. Tel: 0242 577677.

**CHICHESTER**
**Heseltine Moss & Co**
60a North Street, Chichester, W Sussex PO19 1NB. Tel: 0243-786472.

**COLCHESTER**
**E F Matthews & Co**
Colne House, 5 George Street, Colchester CO1 1TR. Tel: 0206-549831.

**COLWYN BAY**
**Penney Easton & Co**
15 Wynnstay Road, Colwyn Bay, N Wales LL29 8NN. Tel: 0492-30354.

**COVENTRY**
**Credit Suisse Buckmaster & Moore**
66 Queens Road, Coventry CV1 3FU. Tel: 0203-25352.

**DORCHESTER**
**Richardson Chubb & Co**
5 High West Street, Dorchester, Dorset DT1 1UJ. Tel: 0305-65252.

**DUNDEE**
**Parsons & Co**
51 Meadowside, Dundee DD1 9PQ. Tel: 0382-21081

**EASTBOURNE**
**Laing & Cruickshank**
12 Gildredge Road, Eastbourne, East Sussex BN21 4RL. Tel: 0323-20893/31656.

## EDINBURGH
**Bell Lawrie & Co**
PO Box 8, Erskine House, 68 Queen Street, Edinburgh EH2 4AE. Tel: 031-225 2566.

**Parsons & Co**
12 Melville Crescent, Edinburgh EH3 7LU. Tel: 031-226 4466.

**Penney Easton & Co**
21 Dublin Street, Edinburgh EH1 3RF. Tel: 031-556 1195.

**Torrie & Co**
6 Hope Street, Edinburgh EH2 4DB. Tel: 031-225 1766.

**Wood Mackenzie Private Client Services Ltd**
Kintore House, 74/77 Queen Street, Edinburgh EH2 4NS. Tel: 031-225 8525.

## EXETER
**Henry J Garratt & Co**
Broadwalk House, Southernhay, Exeter EX1 1TS. Tel: 0392-52679.

**Milton Mortimer & Co**
21 Southernay West, Exeter EX1 1PR. Tel: 0392-76244/58255.

## GLASGOW
**Campbell Neill & Co**
Stock Exchange House, 69 St Georges Place, Glasgow G2 1JN. Tel: 041-248 6271.

**Carswell & Co**
69 St Georges Place, Glasgow G2 1BU. Tel: 041-221 3402.

**Laing & Cruickshank**
De Quincey House, 48 West Regent Street, Glasgow G2 2RB. Tel: 041-333 9323.

**Parsons & Co**
100 West Nile Street, Glagow G1 2QU. Tel: 041-332 8791.

**Penney Easton & Co**
24 George Square, Glasgow G2 1EB. Tel: 041-248 2911.

**Speirs & Jeffrey**
36 Renfield Street, Glasgow G2 1NA. Tel: 041-248 4311.

**Stirling Hendry & Co**
16 Royal Exchange Square, Glasgow G1 3AD. Tel: 041-248 6033.

## GLOUCESTER
**Heseltine Moss & Co**
2 Beaufort Buildings, Spa Road, Gloucester GL1 1XB. Tel: 0452-25444.

## GUERNSEY
**Credit Suisse Buckmaster & Moore (Guernsey) Ltd**
28A Commercial Arcade, St Peter Port, Guernsey. Tel: 0481-710441.

**Sheppards and Chase**
Suite 374E, Hirzel Court, St Peter Port, Guernsey. Tel: 0481-28950.

## HALIFAX
**Broadbridge Lawson & Co**
Fountain Chambers, Fountain Street, Halifax HX1 1LS. Tel: 0422-67707.

## HARROGATE
**Cawood Smithie & Co**
22 East Parade, Harrogate, N Yorkshire HG1 5LT. Tel: 0423-66781/522226.

**Stancliffe Ltd**
Claremont House, Victoria Avenue, Harrogate, N Yorkshire HG1 5QQ. Tel: 0423-66071.

## HARTLEPOOL
**Cawood Smithie & Co**
73 Church Street, Hartlepool, Cleveland TS24 7DN. Tel: 0429-272231/274491.

## HEREFORD
**Henderson Crosthwaite & Co**
27 King Street, Hereford HR4 9BX. Tel: 0432-265647.

**Vivian Gray & Co**
35 Bridge Street, Hereford HR4 9DG. Tel: 0432-53491.

## HORSHAM
**Henderson Crosthwaite & Co**
Central House, Medwin Walk, Horsham RH12 1AG. Tel: 0403-61167.

## HUDDERSFIELD
**Battye, Wimpenny & Dawson**
Woodsome House, Woodsome Park, Fenacy Bridge, Huddersfield HD8 0JG. Tel: 0484-608066.

**Robert Ramsden & Co**
PO Box B16, Estate Buildings (1st Floor), Railway Street, Huddersfield HD1 1NE. Tel: 0484-21501.

## HULL
**Stancliffe Ltd**
Middleton Chambers, Lowgate, Hull, N Humberside HU1 1EA. Tel: 0482-226293/23935.

**Fowler Sutton & Co**
PO Box 10, 35 Bishop Lane, Hull HU1 1NZ. Tel: 0482-25750.

## IPSWICH
**Charles Stanley & Co**
16 Northgate Street, Ipswich, Suffolk IP1 3DB. Tel: 0473-210264.

**Vivian Gray & Co**
23 Lower Brook Street, Ipswich, Suffolk IP4 1AQ. Tel: 0473-225075.

## ISLE OF MAN
**Credit Suisse Buckmaster & Moore (IOM) Ltd**
3 Athol Street, Douglas, Isle of Man. Tel: 0624-27134.

**Ramsey Crookall & Co**
25 Atholl Street, Douglas, Isle of Man. Tel: 0624-73171.

**R L Stott & Co**
Exchange House, 54–58 Athol Street, Douglas, Isle of Man. Tel: 0624-73701.

## JERSEY
**Brewin Dolphin & Co**
Caversham House, 19 Queen Street, St Helier, Jersey. Tel: 0534-27391/2/3

**James Capel (Channel Islands) Ltd**
5 Britannia Place, St Helier, Jersey. Tel: 0534-77077.

**Charlton Seal Dimmock & Co**
Channel House, Green Street, St Helier, Jersey, CI. Tel: 0534-25225.

**Charterhouse-Tilney**
PO Box 348, Charterhouse Building, Bath Street, St Helier, Jersey. Tel: 0534-79437.

**Hoare Govett (Jersey) Ltd**
PO Box 1, 35 Don Street, St Helier, Jersey. Tel: 0534-77548.

**Le Masurier James & Chinn**
PO Box 16, 29 Broad Street, St Helier, Jersey. Tel: 0534-72825.

**Sheppards and Chase**
12 Esplanade, St Helier, Jersey. Tel: 0534-76222.

**Stancliffe Ltd**
Industria House, Red Houses, St Brelade, Jersey. Tel: 0534-45567.

**LANCASTER**
**Hanson & Co**
66 Church Street, Lancaster LA1 1LW. Tel: 0245-32582.

**LEEDS**
**Broadbridge Lawson & Co**
16 Park Place, Leeds LS1 2SJ. Tel: 0532-443721.

**Howitt & Pemberton**
17th Floor, Royal Exchange House, Boar Lane, Box No 85, Leeds LS1 5NS. Also at Stock Exchange, Leeds LS1 5NS. Tel: 0532-439011/450531.

**Redmayne-Bentley**
Merton House, 84 Albion Street, Leeds LS1 6AG. Tel: 0532-436941.

**Rensburg & Co**
11 Park Square East, Leeds LS1 2NG. Tel: 0532-434631.

**Wise Speke & Co**
Provincial House, 28 Albion Street, Leeds LS1 5AL. Tel: 0532-459341.

**LEICESTER**
**Hill Osborne & Co**
Permanent House, Horsefair Street, Leicester LE1 5BU. Tel: 0533-29185.

**Wiltshire Baldwin & Co**
19 The Crescent, King Street, Leicester LE1 6RX. Tel: 0533-541344.

**LINCOLN**
**Hill Osborne & Co**
Royal Insurance Building, Silver Street, Lincoln LN2 1DU. Tel: 0522-28244.

**LIVERPOOL**
**Ashton Tod McLaren**
13 Castle Street, Liverpool L2 4SU. Tel: 051-236 8281.

**Blankstone Sington & Co**
Martins Buildings, 6 Water Street, Liverpool L2 3SP. Tel: 051-227 1381.

**Charterhouse-Tilney**
385 Sefton House, Exchange Buildings, Liverpool L2 3RT. Tel: 052-236 6000.

**Milnes Lumby Bustard**
Martins Building, 4 Water Street, Liverpool L2 3UF. Tel: 051-236 9891.

**Neilson Hornby Crichton & Co**
22 Dale Street, Liverpool L69 2DD. Tel: 051-236 6666.

**Rensburg & Co**
Silkhouse, Tithebarn Street, Liverpool L2 2NH. Tel: 051-227 2030.

**LONDON**
**Astaire & Co Ltd**
117 Bishopsgate, London EC2M 3TD. Tel: 01-283 2081.

**Barclays de Zoete Wedd**
PO Box 188, Ebbgate House, 2 Swan Lane, London EC4R 3TS. Tel: 01-623 4321.

**A J Bekhor & Co**
12a Finsbury Square, London EC2A 1LT. Tel: 01-628 6050.

**Brewin Dolphin & Co**
5 Giltspur Street, London EC1A 9DE. Tel. 01-248 4400.

**Campbell Neill & Co**
City Gate House, 39 Finsbury Square, London EC2A 1PX. Tel: 01-920 9661.

**James Capel & Co**
PO Box 551, 6 Bevis Marks, London EC3A 7JQ. Tel: 01-621 0011.

**Capel Cure Myers**
65 Holborn Viaduct, London EC1A 2EU. Also at the Stock Exchange, London EC2N 1HP. Tel: 01-236 5080.

**Charterhouse-Tilney Ltd**
1 Warnford Court, Throgmorton Street, London EC2N 2AT. Tel: 01-638 0683.

**Chase Manhattan Securities**
PO Box 152, Portland House, 72/73 Basinghall Street, London EC2V 5DP. Tel: 01-606 6622.

**Cobbold & Roach & Co**
66 Cornhill, London EC3V 3NB. Tel: 01-626 1601.

**Coni Gilbert & Sankey**
10 Throgmorton Avenue, Throgmorton Street, London EC2N 2DH. Tel: 01-638 8871.

**T C Coombs & Co**
22 City Road, London EC1Y 2AG. Tel: 01-628 5070.

**County Securities Ltd**
Drapers Gardens, 12 Throgmorton Avenue, London EC2P 2ES. Tel: 01-382-1000.

**Credit Suisse Buckmaster & Moore**
80 Cannon Street, London EC4N 6HH. Tel: 01-588 2868.

**Dennis Murphy Campbell & Co**
2 Russell Row, London EC2V 8BP. Tel: 01-726 8631.

**John M Douglas & Eykyn Brothers**
30 College Street, London EC4R 2TE. Tel: 01-248 4277.

**Dunkley Marshall**
4 London Wall Buildings, London EC2M 5NX. Tel: 01-638 1282.

**Earnshaw, Haes & Sons**
17 Tokenhouse Yard, London EC2R 7LB. Tel: 01-588 5699.

**J M Finn & Co**
Salisbury House, London Wall, EC2M 5TA. Tel: 01-628 9688.

**Foster & Braithwaite**
22 Austin Friars, London EC2N 2BU. Tel: 01-588 6111.

**Henry J Garratt & Co**
34 Copthall Avenue, London EC2R 7BB. Tel: 01-628 9232/9545.

**Godfray Derby & Co**
6 Broad Street Place, London EC2M 7LH. Tel: 01-638 0767.

**Goodbody Dudgeon**
Warnford Court, Throgmorton Street, London EC2N 2AT. Tel: 01-628 4131.

**Vivian Gray & Co**
10 Dominion Street, London EC2M 2UX. Tel: 01-638 2888.

**Greene & Co**
Bilbao House, 36 New Broad Street, London EC4M 9EL. Tel: 01-628 7241.

**W Greenwell Montagu & Co**
Bow Bells House, Bread Street, London EC4M 9EL. Tel: 01-236-2040.

**Greig Middleton & Co**
78 Old Broad Street, London EC2M 1JE. Tel: 01-920 0481.

**Henderson Crosthwaite & Co**
194 Bishopsgate, London EC2M 4LL. Tel: 01-283 8577.

**Heseltine Moss & Co**
3 Trump Street, London EC2V 8DH. Tel: 01-606 1401.

**Hill Osborne & Co**
Warnford Court, Throgmorton Street, London EC2N 2AT. Tel: 01-628 2205.

**Hitchens Harrison & Co**
Bell Court House, 11 Blomfield Street, London EC2M 1LB. Tel: 01-588 5171/1936.

**Hoare Govett Financial Services Ltd**
319/325 High Holborn, London WC1V 7PB. Tel: 01-404 0344.

**Illingworth & Henriques Ltd**
Wardgate House, 59a London Wall, London EC2M 5UA. Tel: 01-638 0801.

**Jacobson Townsely & Co**
4th Floor, Friars House, 39 New Broad Street, London EC2M 1NH. Tel: 01-638 6671.

**Keith Bayley Rogers & Co**
194 Bishopsgate. London EC2M 4NR. Tel: 01-623 2400.

**Kitcat & Aitken**
17th Floor, Stock Exchange, London EC2N 1HB. Tel: 01-588 6280.

**Kleinwort Grieveson & Co**
PO Box 191, 10 Fenchurch Street, London EC3M 3LB. Tel: 01-623 8000.

**Laing & Cruickshank**
Piercy House, 7 Copthall Avenue, London EC2R 7BE. Tel: 01-588 2800.

**Laurence Keen & Co**
Basildon House, 7–11 Moorgate, London EC2R 6AH. Tel: 01-600 9100.

**Laurence Prust & Co**
Basildon House, 7–11 Moorgate, London EC2R 6AH and The Stock Exchange, London EC2N 1HB. Tel: 01-606 6811.

**Le Mare Martin & Co**
City Gate House, 4th Floor, 39 Finsbury Square, London EC2A 1LE. Tel: 01-628 9472.

**Margetts & Addenbrooke**
65 London Wall, London EC2M 5TU. Tel: 01-588 0421.

**Merrill Lynch Ltd**
Merrill Lynch House, 27 Finsbury Square, London EC2A 1AQ. Tel: 01-382 8000.

**L Messel & Co**
1 Finsbury Avenue, London EC2M 2QE. Tel: 01-377 0123.

**Montague Loebl Stanley Financial Services**
31 Sun Street, London EC2M 2QP. Tel: 01-377 9242.

**Murray & Co Stockbrokers**
City Gate House, 39/45 Finsbury Square, London EC2A 1PX. Tel: 01-588 5386/2688.

**Northgate & Co**
119 Finsbury Pavement, London EC2A 1JJ. Tel: 01-628 8121.

**Orme & Co**
Warnford Court, Throgmorton Street, London EC2N 2BD. Tel: 01-638 0991.

**Penney Easton & Co**
3 St Helens Place, London EC3A 6AU. Tel: 01-628 9321.

**Quilter Goodison Co Ltd**
31 Gresham Street, London EC2V 7LH. Tel: 01-600 4177.

**Savory Mill**
3 London Wall Buildings, London EC2M 5PU. Tel: 01-638 1212.

**Schaverien & Co**
18½ Sekforde Street, London EC1R 0HN. Tel: 01-251 1626.

**Paul E Schweder, Miller & Co**
46/50 Sun Street, London EC2M 2PX. Tel: 01-588 5600.

**Albert E Sharp**
6/7 Queen Street, London EC4N 1SP. Tel: 01-248 8678.

**Shaw & Co**
4 London Wall Buildings, Blomfield Street, London EC2M 5NT. Tel: 01-638 3644.

**Sheppards & Chase**
Clements House, Gresham Street, London EC2V 7AU. Tel: 01-606 8099.

**Smith New Court Agency Ltd**
Salisbury House, London Wall, London EC2M 5SX. Tel: 01-628 4433.

**Southard Gilbey McNish & Co**
65 London Wall, London EC2M 5TU. Tel: 01-638 6761.

**Spencer Thornton & Co**
29 Throgmorton Street, London EC2N 2JU. Tel: 01-628 4411.

**Springer Bale & Lewis**
110 Warnford Court, Throgmorton Street, London EC2N 2BB. Tel: 01-628 9941/8322.

**Stancliffe Ltd**
29 Throgmorton Street, London EC2N 2AT. Tel: 01-628 3321.

**Charles Stanley & Co**
18 Finsbury Circus, London EC2M 7BL. Tel: 01-638 5717.

**Sternberg Thomas Clarke & Co**
218 Bishopsgate, London EC2M 4QD. Tel: 01-247 8461.

**Teather & Greenwood**
Austin Friars House, 2–6 Austen Friars, London EC2N 2EE. Tel: 01-628 0321.

**R J Thompson**
1 Salisbury Buildings, London Wall, London EC2M 5RH. Tel: 01-588 2790.

**Helbert Wagg & Co**
(Anderson Bryce Villiers Ltd)
9 Devonshire Square, London EC2M 4YL. Tel: 01-623 4500.

**Walker Crips Weddle Beck & Co**
152 City Road, London EC1V 2PQ. Tel: 01-253 7502.

**Russell Wood & Co**
Kennet House, Kennet Wharf Lane, Upper Thames Street, London EC4V 3AJ. Tel: 01-236 3761.

**Raphael, Zorn**
10 Throgmorton Avenue, London EC2N 2DP. Tel: 01-628 4000.

**LONDONDERRY**
**D M Wright & Partners**
15 The Diamond, Londonderry BT48 6HW Northern Ireland. Tel: 0504-263344.

**MANCHESTER**
**Ashworth Sons & Barratt**
26 Pall Mall, Manchester M2 1LS. Tel: 061-832 4812.

**Bell Houldsworth & Co**
4 Norfolk Street, Manchester M60 2QL. Tel: 061-834 3542.

**Charlton Seal Dimmock & Co**
76 Cross Street, Manchester M60 2EP. Tel: 061-832 3488.

**Henry Cooke Lumsden Ltd**
PO Box 369, 1 King Street, Manchester M60 3AH. Tel: 061-834 2332.

**Gall & Eke**
10 Charlotte Street, Manchester M1 4FL. Tel: 061-228 2511.

**Illingworth & Henriques Ltd**
PO Box 419, 38/40 Kennedy Street, Manchester M60 2BP. Tel: 061-236 8521.

**W H Ireland & Co**
Dennis House, Marsden Street, Manchester M2 1HL. Tel: 061-832 2174/834 6325.

**Piling Trippier & Co**
12 St Anns Square, Manchester M2 7HT. Tel: 061-832 6581.

**John Siddall & Son**
4 Norfolk Street, Manchester M2 1DS. Tel: 061-832 7471.

**Arnold Stansby & Co**
Dennis House, Marsden Street, Manchester M2 3JJ. Tel: 061-832 8554.

**MIDDLESBROUGH**
**Cawood Smithie & Co**
48a High Street, Stokesley, Middlesbrough, Cleveland TS9 5AX. Tel: 0642-712771.

**Stancliffe Ltd**
206 Marton Road, Middlesbrough, Cleveland TS4 2JE. Tel: 0642-249211.

**Wise Speke & Co**
103 Albert Road, Middlesbrough, Cleveland TS1 2PA. Tel: 0642-248431.

**NEWBURY**
**Heseltine Moss & Co**
25 Bartholomew Street, Newbury RG14 5LL. Tel: 0635-37800.

**NEWRY**
**Magennis & Co**
43 Lower Mill Street, Newry BT34 1AH. Tel: 0693-4314.

**NEWCASTLE-UPON-TYNE**
**Penney Easton & Co**
1 Collingwood Buildings, Collingwood Street, Newcastle-upon-Tyne NE1 1JF. Tel: 091-261 9957.

**Wise Speke & Co**
Commercial Union House, 39 Pilgrim Street, Newcastle-upon-Tyne NE1 6RQ. Tel: 091-261 1266.

**NORTHAMPTON**
**Cave & Sons**
9–11 Hazelwood Road, Northampton NN1 1LQ. Tel: 0604-21421.

**NORWICH**
**Barratt & Cooke**
5 Opie Street, Norwich NR1 3DW. Tel: 0603-624236.

**E F Matthews & Co**
5 Queen Street, Norwich NR2 4SG. Tel: 0603-622265.

**NOTTINGHAM**
**William Chapman Trease & Co**
Norwich Union House, South Parade, Nottingham NG1 2LN. Tel: 0602-476772.

**OXFORD**
**Heseltine Moss & Co**
4 King Edward Street, Oxford OX1 4HJ. Tel: 0865-243581.

**PERTH**
**Penney Easton & Co**
4 Charlotte Street, Perth PH1 5LL. Tel: 0738-37441/73817.

**PETERBOROUGH**
**Credit Suisse Buckmaster & Moore**
88 Lincoln Road, Peterborough PE1 2SN. Tel: 0733-311611.

**PLYMOUTH**
**Westlake & Co (Stockbrokers) Ltd**
Princess House, Eastlake Walk, Plymouth PL1 1HG. Tel: 0752-220971.

**POOLE**
**A J Bekhor & Co**
153 High Street, Poole, Dorset BH15 1AU. Tel: 0202-678081.

**Godfray Derby & Co**
38 Parkstone Road, Poole, Dorset BH15 2PG. Tel: 0202-676433.

**READING**
**Helseltine Moss & Co**
30 Friar Street, Reading, Berks RG1 1AH. Tel: 0734-595511.

**SALISBURY**
**Vivian Gray & Co**
45–55 Milford Street, Salisbury, Wiltshire SP1 2BP. Tel: 0722-330333.

**SCARBOROUGH**
**Hill Osborne & Co**
17 York Place, Scarborough YO11 2NP. Tel: 0723-372478.

**SHEFFIELD**
**Nicholson Barber & Co**
PO Box 132, Fargate Court, Fargate, Sheffield S1 1LE. Tel: 0742-755100.

**Walter Ward & Co**
11 Norfolk Row, Sheffield S1 2PA. Tel: 0742-22292.

**SOUTHAMPTON**
**Cobbold Roach & Co**
61 Devonshire Road, Southampton SO9 1XL. Tel: 0703-333292.

**STIRLING**
**Penny Easton & Co**
18 Maxwell Close, Stirling, Scotland SK8 1JU. Tel: 0786 73817.

**STOCKPORT**
**McLellan Ballard & Co**
2–6 Norbury Street, Stockport SK1 3SH. Tel: 061-480 3906/3035.

## STOKE-ON-TRENT
**P H Pope & Son**
6 Pall Mall, Hanley, Stoke-on-Trent. Tel: 0782-251154.

## SUNDERLAND
**Stancliffe Ltd**
57 John Street, Sunderland, Tyne & Wear SR1 1QH. Tel: 0783-657575.

## SWANSEA
**Heseltine Moss & Co**
6 Caer Street, Swansea SA1 1DD. Tel: 0792-54907.

## TAUNTON
**Laing & Cruickshank**
4 Mendip House, High Street, Taunton, Somerset TA1 3SX. Tel: 0823-54351.

## TIVERTON
**Vivian Gray & Co**
The Clock House, East Anstley, Nr Tiverton, Devon EX16 9JB. Tel: 0398-4393.

## TORQUAY
**Whale Hardaway & Co**
5 Parkhill Road, Torquay TQ1 2AN. Tel: 0803-22441.

## TRURO
**Vivian Gray & Co**
Eagle Star House, Lemon Street, Truro, Cornwall TR1 2PX. Tel: 0872-75454.

## TUNBRIDGE WELLS
**T C Coombs & Co**
5 York Road, Tunbridge Wells, Kent TN1 1JX. Tel: 0892-39501.

## WAKEFIELD
**Broadbridge Lawson & Co**
19 King Street, Wakefield WF1 2SP. Tel: 0924-372601/371504.

## WELLS
**Godfray Derby & Co**
Penniless Porch, Market Place, Wells, Somerset BA5 1DJ. Tel: 0749-76373.

## WESTCLIFF-ON-SEA
**Henry J Garratt & Co**
67 Hamlet Court Road, Westcliff-on-Sea, Essex SS0 7EU. Tel: 0702-347173.

## WINCHESTER
**Cobbold Roach & Co**
3 St Peters Street, Winchester, Hants SO23 8BJ. Tel: 0962-52362.

## WORCESTER
**Henderson Crosthwaite & Co**
Virginia House, The Butts, Worcester. Tel: 0905-29551.

## YORK
**Greig Middleton & Co**
23 Petergate, York YO1 2HS. Tel: 0904-647911.

## IRISH REPUBLIC

## CORK
**Beale Sheffield & Co**
15 South Mall, Cork. Tel: 270828/270326.

**Goodbody Dudgeon**
South Mall, Cork. Tel: 965581.

**Maguire McCann Morrison & Co**
12 Marlboro Street, Cork. Tel: 270697.

**W & M Morrogh**
74 South Mall, Cork. Tel: 270647.

## DUBLIN
**Bloxham Toole O'Donnell.**
11 Fleet Street, Dublin 2. Tel: 776653.

**Butler & Briscoe**
3 College Green, Dublin 2. Tel: 777348.

**Campbell O'Connor & Co**
8 Cope Street, Dublin 2. Tel: 771773/771368.

**J & E Davey**
60/63 Dawson Street, Dublin 2. Tel: 772416.

**Doak & Co**
3–5 Suffolk Street, Dublin 2. Tel: 770952.

**Goodbody Dudgeon**
4 College Green, Dublin 2. Tel: 593888.

**McCaw Fleming & Judd**
Aston House, Aston's Place, Dublin 2. Tel: 776941.

**Maguire McCann Morrison & Co**
12 Anglesea Street, Dublin 2. Tel: 771341.

**Moore Gamble Carnegie & Co**
24 Anglesea Street, Dublin 2. Tel: 770572.

**National City Dillon & Waldron Ltd**
Ferry House, 48/53 Lower Mount Street, Dublin 2. Tel: 612944.

**O'Brien & Toole**
2 College Street, Dublin 2. Tel: 778797/778228/778303.

**Porter & Irvine**
18/19 College Green, Dublin 2. Tel: 793715/793582.

**Riada & Co**
28/29 Grafton Street, Dublin 2. Tel: 791411.

**Solomons Abrahamson & Co**
Bank of Ireland Chambers, 1/3 Westmoreland Street, Dublin 2. Tel: 778264/776141.

**Stokes & Kelly Bruce Symes & Wilson**
24 Anglesea Street, Dublin 2. Tel: 770572.

**LIMERICK**
**Maguire McCann Morrison & Co**
46 Cecil Street, Limerick. Tel: 44065.

# Index

Acid test   42
Accountant  55
Account trading   55
After hours deal   55
Allotment letter   55
Annual general meeting (AGM)   55
Annual report & accounts   23, 41, 43, 56
Articles of Association   56
At best deal   53, 56
Auditor's report   41
Authorised capital   58

Balance sheet   23, 56
Ballot   33
Bargain   56
Baring Maurice   27
Bear and bear market   15, 16, 18, 19, 20, 22, 40, 56
Bearer stock   56
Bed & breakfast deal   56
Bid price   56
Big Bang   52, 56
Blue button   57
Blue chip   13, 57
Bonus issue   57
British Gas   34

British Telecom   13, 32, 34, 38
Bull & bull market   15, 18, 19, 20, 22, 40, 49, 57
Business Expansion Scheme   57

Call option   53
Calls   35, 58
Capital   58
Capital assets   41
Capitalisation issue   58
Cash settlement   58
Ceefax   53
Chairman's review   41
Charts   46
Closing   58
Companies register   54
Constant £   44
Constant ratio   45
Contract note   54, 59
Convertible stock   58
Coupon   59
Cover (dividend)   38, 60
Cum dividend   59
Cum rights   59
Cum scrip   59
Current assets   41
Current liabilities   42

Darvas Nicolas   17
Dawn raid   59
Dealing   60
Dealing new time   60
Debenture   60
Depreciation   41, 60
Dividend   38, 60

Earnings per share   60

Equities 45, 60
Ethical Investment Research & Information Service
(EIRIS) 26
Eurobond 61
Ex-dividend 60
Ex-rights 61
Ex-scrip 61
Extel 25
Extraordinary General Meeting 61

Final dividend 61
Financial Times 23, 27, 33, 34, 37, 43
FT Ordinary share index 19, 20, 21, 17, 55, 61
FT 100 share index 20, 61
FT All share index 20, 61
Flotation 61
Formula plan 44
Fully paid 35
Futures 61

Garland Judy 31
Gilts 61
Goodwill 42
Gross interest 62

Hammering 62
Hedge 62

Index linked gilt 62
Institutions 62
Investment club 62
Investment research of Cambridge 47
Investment Trust 62
Investors' Chronicle 37, 43
Issuing House 33

Jevons Professor   19
Jobber   62

Leaders and laggards   27
Leob Gerald M.   21
Letters of Acceptance   35
Limit order   53, 63
Liquidation   63
Listed company   63
Loan capital   58
Long   63

Market-maker   63
Medium term   63
Middle price   63
Millard Brian Investment Services   47

Net asset value   42, 63
Net profit   41
New issues   32, 53, 63
New time   63
Nominee   63
Nominal value   64

Offer price   64
Options   64
Oracle   53
Ordinary share   65
Over the counter (OTC) dealers   52, 53, 65
Oversubscribed   33, 35

Paid-up capital   58
Par   65
Partly paid   65
Penny shares   65
Placing   35, 65

Portfolio   46, 65
Preference shares   65
Prestel   53
Price   38
Price earnings ratio   39, 65
Profits   41
Prospectus   33, 66
Proxy   66

Quick assets ratio   42
Quoted   66

Redemption   66
Redemption yield   66
Renunciation   66
Report & Accounts   41
Return on capital employed   42
Rights issue   35, 36, 66
Rothschild Natham   21
Round figures syndrome   49

Scrip issue   67
Securities   67
Sell in May   49
Selling short   19, 67
Settlement day   67
Share capital   58
Share certificate   54, 67
Share perks   67
Shareholders' funds   42
Shorts   67
Speculation fund   15
Spread   67
Stale bull   67
Stamp duty   14, 67
Stags   32, 35, 67

Stock   42, 67
Stock Transfer form   54
Stockbroker, finding one   51
Stockbroker's commission   14, 52
Stock Exchange   47, 52
Stock Exchange compensation fund   52, 58
Stop-loss system   15
Striking price   68
Sweetener   68
Swings within swings   21
Switch   68

Take-over   31, 34
Tap stock   68
Tip-sheets   28
Tender   34, 68
Traded option   68
TSB (Trustee Savings Bank)   13, 32, 34

Underwriter   68
Unit Trust   13, 68
Unlisted Securities Market (USM)   68
Unsecured Loan stock   69

Variable ratios   46

Wall Street   17
Wall Street crash   19
Warrant   69

Yearlings   69
Yield   38, 69

# WHICH OF THESE FIVE MONEYSPINNING IDEAS WILL HELP YOU MAXIMISE YOUR WEALTH?

WITHIN two months you could be hundreds, even thousands of pounds better off. Simply use one of the moneyspinning ideas listed in the two months trial offer for the MONEY WISE NEWSLETTER and then sit back and watch your family's finances take a turn for the better.

Editor of MONEY WISE NEWSLETTER is David Lewis, who after writing for Money Which? and editing Money Management, was editor of Money Mail for ten years.

If you want to know more about the special offer of two months' free trial, just cut out the coupon below – or if you don't want to cut your book just send your name and address without obligation to MONEY WISE NEWSLETTER, Dept SH, FREEPOST, London NW3 1YP. You need not put a stamp on your envelope – we will even pay the postage.

---

**Send today for details of the free trial offer**
To: Money Wise Newsletter, Dept SH,
FREEPOST, London NW3 1YP

Please send me details of the Two Months Trial Offer for the Money Wise Newsletter edited by David Lewis. I understand that I am under no obligation.

Name
_____
BLOCK CAPITALS PLEASE
Address
_____
BLOCK CAPITALS PLEASE

_____

_____

Postcode

See order form overleaf

**For Your Notes**

**For Your Notes**

# For Your Notes

# For Your Notes

# For Your Notes

**For Your Notes**